ALL IN YOUR HEAD

Victoria Wright

To Isabella, William and Niamh, I love you xxx

Jenny, Martin and Toni thank you for all your support in writing this and to my friends and family for your ongoing support xxx

CONTENTS

Introduction

Growing up in a competitive environment is tough, both my parents frequently played sports and worked incredibly hard their entire lives. My father was the son of a coal miner but in business has achieved huge amounts of success. He was and still is always inspiring to be around, not just for his own family but for other people too. I grew up watching people idolise and respect him in whatever he did as he took on more and more responsibilities. A strong work ethic was driven into me and my two sisters from a young age, along with financial responsibility from my mother. I desperately wanted to be successful in business and follow in the success that he had had.

The problem is, if someone is successful, they are seen as privileged. Nobody looks at the years of graft or the personal sacrifices made along the way. There's an element of human nature to be jealous of success and to take a kind of cruel joy in looking for faults and negatives. There were many weeks I didn't see my father growing up as he was often away working, but we always understood that what he did was for the good of the family. When he was home, our house was filled with 'I love yous' and my parents always gave us the belief anything was possible. Yes they could be tough but we were encouraged to be worldly and prepared for anything and it's probably thanks to them I'm able to cope with what I have so far.

Despite not being from a horsey background, I was obsessed with horses from a very young age and knew that that was a career path I always wanted to take. After working for different riders and gaining experience, I had a passion for breeding after spending time in Germany. Myself and my father had also developed a shared passion for the sport of three day Eventing and this was something we would become very heavily involved in. It became our time together; something that brought us closer and his switch off from work. We lived in the Nottinghamshire village of Caunton which would later become the prefix to all of our horses, including the ones we bred. It was through the start of Caunton that I also met my future husband Matthew.

Matthew represented Great Britain at Junior, Young Rider and Senior level and was tipped to be the Andy Murray of the Eventing world. He was a phenomenal horseman so it was always hard not to be in awe of him, despite thinking he was an absolute asshole most of the time, a trait I think so common in many elite sportspeople. He lived only thirty minutes away from us so it was an obvious choice to support him as our local event rider to professionally ride and produce our horses in the sport. He had lived in the village of Lound with his parents all his life where they had their own Eventing and horse sales (or dealing yard as it was called). He was under enormous amounts of pressure to keep the family business alive, along with keeping horse owners happy and the good results constantly coming in. In the sport he heavily relied on the support of owners to purchase top horses for him to compete and help with the astronomical running costs in keeping them at the top level. He wasn't from a wealthy background and had got to where he had by horse dealing, his talent and the family's sheer hard work. We always got on well and I was his go to as a person he could really trust when there was a situation he couldn't tell anyone else about. I think from the start of our friendship, silence was something that was drilled into me because of the loyalty I felt towards him. Despite it taking some time and a few bumps along the way, we would inevitably end up together and run the Caunton operation from his yard in Lound. The decision was then taken to swerve away from horse dealing and move to building a stud operation that would house stallions for breeding and allow Matthew to focus on his career competing and build a string of top horses.

We shared three young children together, Isabella, William and Niamh and I still maintain that Matthew was always at his absolute happiest when he was being Daddy. School runs were his favourite part of the day, taking in the eye candy of MILF's and yummy mummies and the weekends spent dragging the kids around on ponies were his favourite. However, living with him day in day out I saw the act; the constant bravado he would put on in front of everyone. He thought it was needed to keep the owners happy and business afloat, to hide the shell of a man he actually felt on the inside.

Having achieved great amounts of success at such a young age, he was under constant expectation from everyone around him and when he wasn't at the top of his game he would instantly feel like a failure. He chased adrenaline to give him a fix and suffered from addictions along the way. He was always an all or nothing person and together we found ways to manage and tackle these problems. For a few years things improved massively and the good days in Matthew's head seemed to outweigh the bad ones. But it was always more than that; I'm sure now there was a chemical imbalance or a severe case of bipolar that was never acknowledged or dealt with. Combined with constant pressure and expectations this was always going to escalate and spiral out of control. When days were good, they were really good, but when they were bad they were darker than you could have ever imagined. Suicide had been something that crossed Matthew's mind whenever he hit rock bottom and is something that had had to be prevented several times. He used to take himself off without telling anyone where he'd gone, just a text to say 'I love you and goodbye.' I'd spent many nights driving around to find him, picking him up from the side of train tracks, talking him down from bridges and calming him down from a complete rage. But I could always level him again or slay off the dragon to free him from the tower his brain had locked him in.

The equestrian industry is tough and a hard sport to be involved in. It's not like you can ever just walk out of the office at 5:30pm or off the pitch and back to your home away from the crowds. You're looking after animals and its frequent long hours, constant requests and daily pressures financially, physically and mentally. During the three-day Eventing season, the early morning starts regularly commence at 2 or 3am and often involve not getting back to the yard until late. When it's your own yard, reputation, and business it doesn't just stop when you get home either, there's never a day off like you'd get if you were working for someone else. I think all of these constant pressures affected his mood and frame of mind as there were some days I struggled to just talk him into getting out of bed to face the world.

I kept quiet for the entire time I was in a relationship and married to Matthew. I brushed it under the carpet, stuck a plaster on it and found myself constantly trying to smooth things over in my mind. It can take its toll on you and there's nothing to be ashamed of in admitting that. It's a snowball effect or avalanche in some cases. It's easy for me to preach now the importance of talking or reaching out if you're struggling or looking after someone who's struggling, after all I'd be telling you to do something that I couldn't do for myself. The biggest question I often think about is "why the hell is it so hard to say anything and why did I never do it?" For me it was the fear of what everyone would think, the things people would say and the judgments they would make. We say we're not, but everyone can be judgmental and we can often do it without even thinking about it, me included;

"You shouldn't stand for that Tor, he's putting you through hell."

"He's not wired up right."

"I can't watch you go through this anymore, you should just leave."

These are all comments I've heard over the years and in certain circumstances people were right to have those opinions. But when you love someone you want to help or cure them in any way you can. "In sickness and in health remember" is what I always used to say to Matthew and mental health is a sickness. They have good days and bad days and you never quite know which personality you're going to wake up with until that morning. I would wake up anxious as to which version of my husband I'd get that day. But when it was a good day, I'd feel ecstatic and like our whole world was back to normal again. On those days when everything is back to normal you want to enjoy them so much and you need your family and friends to act completely normal too. But if they knew all the ins and outs, the ups and downs of the dark days, some people wouldn't have treated him in the same way again. It's easier to only ever speak of the good days and let the bad ones be between you and the four walls witnessing them.

I think it's also a desperation to want to get the person you fell in love with back; to release them from this monster that's possessed them. You only ever want to speak of the good things because it's a reminder to yourself of the good person that's in there that you're desperately trying to find again. Knowing what I know now having lost someone to mental illness, the worst thing I ever did was cover it up. At the time the arguments we would have often featured the words, "If anyone realises how crazy I am, they'll section me!" You know what? Looking back now, it could have been the best thing to have happened and would probably be a very different story today.

When darkness has surrounded the person suffering, they don't want to find any light. They are in a self-loathing, self-destructive spiral and they won't look for any help independently when they are in that frame of mind. It's also very easy in that situation where someone close to you keeps threatening with suicide but doesn't go through with it to become complacent and think that they never actually will. The truth is, nobody knows if someone is actually capable to ever go through with something like that until it's too late. I'm guilty of that and it is a guilt that I will carry for the rest of my life.

"Grief is like the ocean; it comes on waves ebbing and flowing. Sometimes the water is calm, and sometimes it is overwhelming. All we can do is learn to swim."

- Vicki Harrison -

The Darkest Day

For the first couple of months after losing Matthew, life was a little bit like an hourglass. The sand would get to the end and then you'd just turn it round again, a little bit unaware of what day it was, only that the dark indicated night time therefore the end of another day. I threw myself into work and needed distractions and friends around me. I had lost a lot of closeness with my friends through Matthew's depression so socialising again was like a massive surge of endorphins. When you have a bereavement in your family or you lose someone close to you, I don't think it's the first week it hits you being alone, it's the first month when everyone has gone and continued to live their own lives again. That's when you have the out of body experience of "Fuuuuuck, it's actually just me now!!" In my case I was now both Mum and Dad and responsible for everything. I always used to think I did most things with the kids anyway; like putting them to bed, dressing, changing, bath time, story time and homework. But you then appreciate the things that the other person did even more, the stupid shit; putting petrol in the car, screen wash, nipping to the shop when you're out of milk and doing the cooking.

You then start to feel enormous amounts of pressure, especially as you can see your children grieving themselves to not put yourself into a risky situation that could lead to you getting hurt or taken away from them. You also feel a huge amount of pressure to be strong and appear tough to get them through each day. For those who have lost a partner not just to mental health, but to an accident or other illness, playing both mum and dad is tough and it's easy to neglect yourself to make sure whatever spare time you have is spent on your kids.

My worst trait now is with food. With the exceptions of eating out on some nights and takeaways of course, I cook for the children. Something balanced that they'll actually eat. It always then seems completely pointless to make something for myself so I just eat whatever they've left on their plate, followed by a yoghurt if I'm feeling adventurous. I'm also a dab hand at fuel roulette and realise the lack of inspiration I get at a fuel pump is the reason the responsibility was taken away from me in the first place. A Jerry can in my boot is now top of my Christmas list!

If I said I hadn't had disturbed sleep as a result of everything I'd be a complete liar. I try and keep flashbacks out of my head as I'm a firm believer that the mind is a powerful tool and it can only affect us if we allow it. I'm not a negative person and never have been, my glass is always half full and I'd always rather try and turn something negative into something positive. You can create bad habits for yourself very easily and I've seen that first hand living with someone who constantly let their mind get the better of them. You have to be very blunt with yourself; there's no monster in the dark and I'll only see and remember things if I allow myself too. I got into a habit of working at night on my laptop or reading a book and found it was a great way to switch my mind off and feel tired.

I can still describe the whole night in detail to the minute - The last time I saw Matthew and the last look in his eye alive. About three months prior to his passing we had finally completed on a new equestrian property in the same village we were living in that would be an expansion for the stud business. It had taken quite a while to get the ball rolling as things were moving a lot slower than usual due to the Covid pandemic, but houses were still selling and the property market seemed to be doing quite well. Although we sold our old house, we decided to keep the old yard for the young horses and stud but would eventually move all the stallions and competition horses to the new site once we'd settled into living there ourselves. The house is upside down, with the kitchen and living room upstairs and the bedrooms down. As a converted barn, the ceilings upstairs are high and supported by large beams throughout in an open plan kitchen and living room and a separate main bedroom.

Matthew was a foodie through and through and his passion was to cook, but not just normal meals, with his standards he could have worked in a three Michelin restaurant. He was always very good at throwing anything together, but believe it or not at the start of our relationship he let me cook each night for a year and a half! We were invited one evening to the theatre in London to watch Thriller and knowing how much he loved food I decided to book us into a very good restaurant. That was our first tasting menu experience and after that his mind was blown and I was demoted to pot washer. The kitchen utensils from then on consisted of pasta makers, Thermomixes, sous vide machines and vac pacs. That particular night was Valentine's Day and we'd sat down to enjoy a home delivery tasting menu as we were still in National lockdown at the time; this one in particular was by Marcus Wareing.

While we were eating dinner Matthew said to me; "We've done some amazing things together haven't we?"

"Amazing things and experiences," I said. He tapped the wine glass in front of him with his wedding ring, his usual signal he used that indicated to top up his drink. Anyone who knew Matthew was very familiar with this sound, especially anyone who had worked at the local pub. I filled his glass up across the table and he looked me in the eye drawing more attention to his wedding ring. "If anything ever happens to me, never take off your wedding ring."

I tried to keep the tone light-hearted as he could often turn situations quite dark. "What a lovely direction this conversation's going in."

We laughed and talked about the business, the yard and the direction we wanted things to go in. When Matthew was fun, he was the life and soul of any party, and he was also full of confidence after losing a significant amount of weight and enjoyed showing me that afternoon how all his suits and outfits from when he was twenty-five fitted him again. Whilst we were choosing something to wear for our Valentines date, he took particular pleasure in showing me his favourite suit that fitted him like a glove again, this was something I would soon learn the significance of.

One of my best friends and absolute rock Martin had had the kids for us at his cottage next door and brought them back with the cakes that they'd made that evening. I sat downstairs talking to him for a while whilst the kids ran upstairs to show Daddy their creations, Matthew had poured himself a glass of whiskey and resumed his favourite position on the sofa whilst asking the kids what ingredients they'd used to bake the cakes. After talking to Martin for a while I shouted the kids for bedtime and locked the front door as Martin left. I sat on Bella's bed that evening and, while they nodded off I sat as we all do so often, just scrolling through Facebook on my phone. As the children's eyes closed, the house seemed quiet...eerily quiet. I don't know why but I looked on my own Facebook and noticed posts I had been tagged in with Matthew were gone. The hairs on the back of my neck stood up and I felt cold, my stomach wrapped itself up into a knot and something just felt 'wrong'. I walked up the stairs and glanced at the sofa to see a half drank glass of whiskey placed on the arm and Masterchef on the television with no sign of Matthew. I turned to see the light on in the bedroom and the door half open with a strange shadow across the floor.

"Matthew." I paused a moment. No answer.

The walk I did into the bedroom that night will haunt me for the rest of my life and is a scenario I will replay repeatedly in my mind. As I crept around the corner I could see the bed in front of me, the shadow on the floor grew in darkness and as I glanced up there it was; horror, fear and a worst nightmare in front of my very eyes. Matthew was hanging there; suspended from the beams by his neck with his favourite belt.

Screaming, I jumped onto the bed to reach the beam to try to release the belt and couldn't, his eyes were bloodshot and tongue and face bright blue. I pulled on the belt buckle unsuccessfully several times as I dialled 999. The emergency responder answered and tried to instruct me until the emergency services arrived. I pleaded with them to send someone to 'HELP ME!' Calmly the responder asked me to try and get him down and eventually I managed to release the belt from around his neck. The loud bang onto the floor when he fell from the beam sent shivers down my spine, especially knowing my children heard that too. I heard Bella scream, and I cried out "STAY IN YOUR ROOM!"

I tried to resuscitate Matthew unsuccessfully and followed the instructions of the emergency responder and kept trying to perform CPR on his chest. The ambulance arrived and I ran to the door to let them in and take them upstairs. While the crew tended to him, I rushed quickly back down into Bella's bedroom where she was sat on her bed, cradling her brother and sister in her arms who had gone to her in fear, crying. William asked; "Mummy, why are there so many flashing lights outside?"

"There's nothing to be scared of baby, please just go back to sleep." I walked back upstairs to my bedroom and was greeted by the female police offer who told me to sit on the sofa and not to go back into the bedroom while everyone was in there. I couldn't even bring myself to walk any further than that and just crumpled on the top step of the stairs. I could hear the machines beeping, the emergency workers constantly trying to resuscitate him. I sat there praying to God to 'please, please, please save him'. Eventually…I heard the beeping stop.

Matthew was pronounced dead after thirty two minutes of trying.

The female police officer asked me to come and sit down on the sofa, followed closely behind by the ambulance crew. I knew exactly what they were going to tell me, what I already knew when I was doing the CPR. Hearing the words "I'm very sorry…." followed by "died" was something that made me break in every way physically possible that night. The officer asked if there was anyone who could come and support me so went round to the cottage next door to fetch Martin. Martin came into the living room and threw his arms around me while the tears just kept flooding out. Martin called Matthew's parents and my parents to come round. Time felt like it was stood still, and I couldn't believe this was actually happening. Before the ambulance crew left, they made sure Matthew was comfortable and ready for the undertakers to come and collect him. Matthew's mother Jane arrived alone as his father was incredibly ill at the time, followed by my parents who only had questions to ask, the answers for which I didn't even have myself.

I was allowed to say goodbye to Matthew for one last time. The female police officer took my hand and took me back into the bedroom. Matthew was laid on a pillow on the floor where I left him, peaceful and still. I remember the look on his face and in his eye. It was like the weight of the world was lifted from his shoulders and he was ten years younger. The only comfort I can find in any of it was the look on his face and that he finally looked at peace. I hugged him for one last time and kissed his forehead. His hands were like icicles when I picked them up and removed his wedding ring. "Until death do us part remember." I kissed his forehead again and told him that I would look after our children. My father pulled me away as the undertakers arrived to remove him, I just remember crying hysterically and not wanting him to go.

Dad sat me back down on the sofa and Martin wrapped his arms around me again. The thought that my husband was now being placed into a body bag because I had failed to go upstairs fifteen minutes earlier was a thought I just couldn't stomach, the whole thing felt like the world's worst nightmare. Tears were impossible to fight back as his body was carried down the stairs in a black bag and the last essence of his physical being gone.

The Morning After

The female police officer gave Martin her number as she left, and told him to call if we needed anything; "Anything at all", she said. Her kindness that night is something I will never forget. I remember my father taking control of the situation and telling Martin and Jane to go home and get some sleep and that he and my mother would stay in the spare room downstairs. He told me to try and get some sleep until the morning and rest, but I don't think my eyelids ever shut that night. I laid on Matthew's side of the bed with his dressing gown draped over me counting every second and minute until the clock reached the next hour. I felt totally responsible for his death and couldn't believe I hadn't seen any warning signs this time. I felt like I'd failed him.

As it got near 5am, I sent a message to House Hayley who helps me with the children and has been a huge rock for my family. The name House Hayley was started by my children because we have two very important Hayley's in our lives and it's the easiest way for them to differentiate the two.

"When you wake up, please can you call me, something really bad has happened."

It didn't take long for Hayley to call me and as I answered I felt a huge lump appear in my throat. This was the first phone call I had had to make with the news and it made it feel even more real. I wanted her to come over and take care of the children and try to give them as normal a day as possible whilst we sorted the aftermath out.

"Hayley I'm sorry it's so early but please can you come round as soon as you can, something really bad has happened."

"Of course, I'm on my way."

No questions even asked. I seemed to end up at the top of my stairs again waiting for Hayley to arrive. 5:05, 5:06, 5:07; you spend a lot of time just counting down the minutes. When Hayley eventually walked through the door she looked up at me from the bottom of the stairs where I hadn't moved since the phone call and I started to cry.

"Matthew's dead."

I remember the look of sheer horror on her face as she put her hands over her mouth in disbelief. She shook her head as she came towards me and threw her arms around me. When the door opens in the house it makes a beeping sound which had also woken up the children. Another lump in my throat followed by the feeling I was about to throw up. I knew what I was going to have to do next.

We had tried to keep the children in their bedrooms that night despite them seeing blue flashing lights through the curtains, but the following morning they knew something was desperately wrong. The three of them came hand in hand down the corridor where I greeted them by the front door. I knelt and put my arms around them, pulling them in as tight as I could.

"Babies, I've got something to tell you."

They hugged each other tight and looked at me with a look of worry on their faces.

"Daddy was very poorly last night and had to be taken to the hospital." William looked at floor and Bella's eyes started to fill with tears knowing what was coming next. Telling my kids that Daddy had died was by far the hardest thing I've ever had to do. The sheer devastation on their faces but also knowing that nothing had properly sunk in yet because they were far too young to comprehend what I was telling them. All I knew was this was going to be a very bumpy road ahead.

As Hayley took the children upstairs to get breakfast and they had the happily distracting novelty of seeing my parents whom they'd not seen for a while because of Covid. I walked from the front door into William's bedroom to sit in silence for a while before having to make the next phone call. It was the reality again of having to pick up a phone and say your thirty-eight year old husband is dead without being able to say 'there's been an accident' or 'he's had a heart attack'. All that was going through my head was I could have saved him.

That's what I think is the hardest part of losing a loved one to suicide, the fact you can't give a logical explanation for it. With a heart attack, cancer or car accident you can process it eventually over time in your head as an act of God, something that couldn't be helped. It's difficult to process the thought that the person you loved ended their own life and that if you had gone upstairs fifteen minutes earlier you could have stopped them.

The next call always needed to be to Matthew's best friend Matt, a fellow three-day event rider and someone he communicated with hundreds of times a day. I dialled his number and he didn't answer the first time, but immediately called back confused as to why I'd called him at such an early hour.

"Matthew's gone," was all I could bring myself to say.

"What do you mean he's gone Tor?"

"He's dead."

There it was, that word again and that gut wrenching reality feeling right there. Matt was silent on the phone for a few minutes as there were literally no words he could find. "I'll be there as soon as I can, we'll leave in the next hour." I could hear the sadness in Matt's voice on the phone.

With some incredibly difficult hurdles crossed, there was the final one still to go; everyone at the yard. I sent a message to Yard Hayley, another loyal member of the family to come to the house before she went into the yard that morning. As soon as I knew she was on the way I sat waiting by the front door for her to arrive. As she pulled up I ran onto the drive to greet her at her passenger door. Now the children were awake I didn't want them to hear too much. Hayley knew something was desperately wrong and looked incredibly concerned as she unlocked her passenger door for me to climb in.

"I was too late" I cried. The tears flooded out again and Hayley confused, wrapped her arms around me.

"What's happened? What's wrong?"

"Matthew's dead, he killed himself." That sentence made me feel sick.

Hayley started to cry herself and we just sat holding each other as tightly as we could. After finding some composure, I asked her to let the others at the yard to know what had happened and to sort the horses as usual. By the time Matt had arrived, in the space of two hours the horse world and village jungle drums of gossip had swung into full action and his phone never stopped ringing.

"I've heard he's shot himself."

"Is it true he took an overdose?"

All of these were comments that were made, rumours that were passed on and Matthew's past of finding trouble wherever he went resurfaced to haunt him one last time. Yes, he had had a tough exterior, but nobody really knew him on the inside and just how soft he actually was. I still find it disturbing as to why some people tried to find out the gory details or fabricate on them like it was a horror film. That horror film was currently my life and one I was trying to protect my children from.

As the phone continued to ring and following some sound advice from a good friend, we decided to put a statement out on social media to confirm the news:

"The horse world is a small and close community, and we are aware that people are already starting to hear the sad news about Matthew. It is with great sadness that we have to confirm that this is true. Matthew has always been open with everyone about his own battles with mental health and has worked hard to support others through their own. Please could we ask that you respect the family's privacy and give us the opportunity to grieve at this difficult time."

After we put out the post I turned my phone onto aeroplane mode and between Matt, my sister Alex and Matthew's other close friend Angus they started to deal with the aftermath. Alex took me in her car down to the old yard to visit the horses and show my face to the whole team. I'd put Matthew's wedding ring over the top of mine to make sure I gave all of the horses one last pat from him with it. At the time this made me feel like I was connecting him to them in some way. The biggest pats and tears went to his two favourite horses, Comfort and Amy.

Members of the team greeted me with hugs and said they would do anything they could to help and that we would get through all of this together. Although Matthew was always a hard person to work for; his standards were high and he was strict on routine. He was remarkable with the horses and the team had enormous amounts of respect for him as a horseman and instantly missed his guidance. To keep going was a promise I made to them all but at the time, with a yard full of competition horses that owners and family had invested in and a brand-new set up, it was a promise I made through gritted teeth.

Although lots of family and friends were supportive, there were also lots of questions that followed, along with accusations and blame that those people felt needed to be made. The fact what had happened had happened, was something that a lot of people couldn't come to terms with, mainly because I had also kept a lot of the troubles to myself over the years. I remember some of the comments;

"There's got to be more to this, he wouldn't just do something like that. It doesn't make any sense."

"Matthew was strong, I can't see him just deciding to do that."

 I caught people scrolling through messages on my phone, messages that were private but also weren't going to give anyone any answers. I felt like through everyone else's shock and grief they needed to place blame or believe there was something more to it that had gone on and the obvious person to blame or presume was hiding answers was me.

So many people were visiting the house, close friends but also people I hadn't seen in years that I felt had turned up to get the lowdown on the drama. I didn't know where to put myself as I know a lot of people were being supportive but equally you just wanted to be shut away from the world and just with the people who truly understood. Matt took me for a walk around the fields to help me to clear my head and prepare me for what was to come next.

The Aftermath

Following the death of a loved one, relative or friend in a normal circumstance; the day after we are encouraged to be around our family and friends to grieve and come to terms with the sadness. After a suicide it is very different and I can give a first-hand comparison on that as a few months later in 2021, Matthew's father Rodger also passed away from cancer.

Following a suicide, you are left in what feels like a crime scene, your loved one's phone and electronic devices are taken away in an evidence bag and the police return twenty four hours later for questioning. The whole thing becomes part of an inquest that includes toxicology reports and the coroner's court. Because we were still in lockdown, the inquest wasn't going to be quick which meant there was going to be some delay until the funeral could actually take place.

When the police arrived two officers turned up in an unmarked car and myself and Matt greeted them in Martin's cottage so we were out of earshot of the children. They needed to take an official statement and wanted me to go through the whole evening in detail once again. You feel like they are cross examining you, especially in the circumstances of it happening in our own home. Enormous waves of guilt kept rushing through my body.

"It's my fault, I can't believe I didn't go upstairs. It was just so quiet; I didn't hear anything and he'd been the happiest he'd ever been. I let him die."

As I sat with my head in my hands the officers were kind and told me not to think like that and that during lockdown the suicide rate had been incredibly high, but it didn't matter what anyone said at this stage. The whole thing was so confusing, Matthew had been the happiest I'd ever known him. We had just moved house to what he described was the place of his dreams, we had good horses for him to compete and he was the fittest and most focused he'd been for a very long time.

Other close friends also turned up that afternoon, so House Hayley's partner Chris, Yard Hayley's Alex, Matt, Angus and Martin decided to do a recce in the afternoon for any notes or signs of anything that Matthew could have left lying around the place to give us answers. When they returned after an hour, huddled together in a small group they struggled to find the words to tell me that they had found a lunge line taken from the yard into the horsebox and turned into what resembled a noose.

About a month prior Matthew had acted incredibly strange one evening and began to cry when the song 'The Sound of Silence' by Disturbed was played on Spotify. He disappeared that same evening for a couple of hours in the rain following an argument about a coat I'd melted a part of by standing too close to the fire. When his personality used to switch, he could start an argument about absolutely anything and you were always better to not retaliate. There was no I'm sorry or I love you text or telling me has was going to do something stupid like he often did, he just said he was going to the yard. When he returned, he got back into bed and apologised as we had a rule we would never go to bed on an argument, kissed me and went to sleep. It hit me there and then. That's where he'd gone that evening and he'd thought about it then but unlike any other time never said anything about it. You then start to question how long he'd been planning it for, especially when we also realised he'd chopped a years' worth of fire wood for the house.

The first night after, I was adamant that I needed to sleep in my own bed to not make an issue about my bedroom in my own mind. The room was a crime scene less than twenty-four hours earlier but it needed to be just my bedroom again now.

"You don't need to go back in there tonight." Martin said. "There's no shame in that, you don't have to do it if you don't want to."

"No! I need to, I have to go back in there."

I was so determined so Yard Hayley said to me; "Come on, you don't have to do this on your own. If you're going to do it you need a spooning buddy."

After Martin had cooked dinner for everyone and I had pushed the food around my plate unable to stomach anything yet, we put the bedside lights on and changed into our pyjamas whilst Martin, Matt and Angus sat in the kitchen. My mother had also stayed and taken the children to bed with her in William's room so she could comfort them. As soon as night fell, they started to panic that the blue flashing lights would come back and claim another victim.

We got into bed and Hayley put her arm out for me to cuddle up to her.

"Can we keep the light on?"

"Absolutely, we can keep all of the lights on if you need to."

I snuggled more into her arm and took in a deep breath as my eyes glanced up to look at the beam. I felt the hairs on the back of my neck stand up and let out a gasp of sheer terror.

"Hayley! Oh my god! He's written on the fucking beam!"

I started to breathe rapidly. She looked up at the beam too and held me tightly but was also equally horrified. We heard the kitchen chairs move swiftly as they heard the commotion from the bedroom and I rapidly shot into the kitchen with my hands firmly fixed on the top of my head.

"He's written on the beam!" I cried out as I was placed on a kitchen chair and told to sit down. Matt and Angus made their way into the bedroom before coming out, closing the door behind them, and carrying a rug out of it that still had blood on it that had spilled out of Matthew's nose and mouth the night before.

"Don't go back in there." They said angrily. Anger was an emotion quite a few people felt and one that a lot of family members can feel after someone has taken their own life. The instruction was very clear as was the message on the beam.

'Brooks was here'

This was the same message written on the beam in The Shawshank Redemption, a film Matthew had made me watch again a few days prior, it appeared parts of the puzzle were starting to fit together.

The police had to come back again the following day to view the evidence and again take further statements and photos before giving permission to have the message removed. They recommended having the beam sand blasted down so my good friend Kate called in a favour the next day so we could open the door to that room again. When the message was removed, Kate had opened all the windows and placed two vases of fresh flowers by the side of my bed to make it more enticing to be back in there. By this point I'd already started sleeping downstairs in Bella's room and close friends kindly stayed with me for the first two weeks on a rota between Yard Hayley, House Hayley, Martin, Matt, Jenny and Kate so I didn't have to be in the house alone.

I felt instantly the general expectation from everyone was that I was going to quit. I know family members were trying to be supportive, but ultimately they are also presuming you're weak. I got told on several occasions; "It's ok to go back home to Caunton." Or "What are you going to do now, sell up? What's going to happen with everything?" There were so many people relying on me to make a decision - It was a big weight on my shoulders seeing people depend on me to keep going, but it was also a motivating factor that nearly all of them had presumed I was going to just quit. I don't think they thought I'd be able to stay in the house anymore and would just want to sell up. This fuelled the fire i me and I felt charged up. Why should I stop o _ because that's what other people would do? We moved here because of all the opportunities it presented, it's a beautiful place and I can fucking do this.

It's amazing during the madness of grief when people want to help you but don't know what to do that food and flowers seem to be everybody's go to. I had enough meals, giant lasagnes, cottage pies, bunches of flowers and Sunday lunches to feed the five thousand and I will never be able to thank everybody enough for their kindness during that time. Weirdly the go to for my mother and sister was John Lewis toilet roll holders that they decided needed to go in each bathroom. The van pulled up outside and I thought 'more flowers or food parcels', but no, three boxes in I'd realised everyone had got fed up with having to stretch or lean to wipe their arse!

The Madness Of Grief

The first week was a total blur, I remember the house being full of visitors and sitting on the wooden floor in the kitchen against the wall with my brother-in-law Chris cleaning out the fridge and fixing a leak under my sink. Everything in the fridge, freezer and cupboards being placed on the kitchen island felt overwhelming.

Truffle oil

Balsamic glaze

Scallops

Squid

Matthew could cook and most meals resembled a Michelin starred restaurant as opposed to my basic pub grub that was usually centred around beef mince. What the fuck am I actually going to do with all of this stuff? If I'd tried to put it all together I'd have made something like Rachel's dessert on Friends, half a Shepherd's Pie and half a trifle!

Despite spending the week in much of a trance, it's weird the stuff you remember like that, the standout moments that trigger your memory. I remember the moments that made me smile like being helped to have a bath by my girlfriends because it was quite a task going back into my bedroom and I didn't want to be alone. As they washed my hair we said "You silly bastard, you'd have killed to have been watching this right now!"

And I remember the moments that would instantly make me cry, like when my sister found a note that Bella had written in her bedroom to Daddy;

"Please come back Daddy, it's not the same without you. I miss you so so much. Please Daddy come back."

This broke me into a million pieces all over again and what made it worse was that she couldn't speak to me about it because she knew I was so broken she didn't want to upset me. I went upstairs to find Bella sat on the sofa and sat at the side of her. She cuddled me and said "Don't worry Mummy, I'll look after you." That was it right there, that was the switch. The trance was broken and I felt the biggest invisible slap across my face.

"No baby, it's my job to look after you and that's exactly what Mummy's going to do." Being the eldest of three siblings meant that it was always Bella that most jobs fell onto. "Bella, please can you pass me the baby wipes." When you're in the middle of changing her younger brother or sister. "Bella, just open the door and let the dogs out." We had always unintentionally put pressure on her shoulders to help look after the other two and be the responsible role model to them. In doing this she was always seeking praise and approval, especially from her Daddy.

I couldn't sit there on the floor and rock in the corner anymore. I had an eight, five and four year old who needed a Mummy and needed a Mummy more than ever. They were broken too and in need of more answers than anyone else did. What made it worse was that the answers they needed they wouldn't be able to get until they are old enough to understand.

The horses were still living at the old yard and the yard at our new home was still in need of repair and a good clean up. The tack room was knocked down and just a brick shell with a puddle of water on the floor in the middle of it. I got it into my head that I needed the horses at the new yard straight away, I couldn't oversee everything even if they were only a short drive away while the kids were at home and homeschooling. So what do you do when you're grieving? In my case take on the biggest tasks you can find.

I knew this was going to be one hell of a job and I couldn't do this alone. I got in touch with old school friends who I knew were joiners, electricians, or just practical and handy to call in some favours. The whole team at the yard also turned up to grab a paintbrush and get stuck into the tidy up mission. I think I must have made about twenty-two trips to the builders merchants for more masonry paint, but once we started we weren't stopping. On the third visit after ordering yet again more paint, I rocked up in black jeans plastered in white paint and a pair of ankle boots also white accompanied by dried white paint strands in my hair. The cashier looked at me after having served me previously the day before. The dark circles under my eyes must have made him think I was going at it hard all night.

"What are you painting love? The Great Wall Of China?"

"Something like that."

I sighed as it certainly felt like a never ending task at the time. We bundled the paint in the boot of the car, and it felt like a rush to get back to the yard and get going again. I couldn't stop, I'm impulsive anyway and when I want something I want it yesterday, especially when people were telling me to slow down and it wasn't possible in that amount of time. That just drives me even more. Within three weeks of Matthew's passing and before the funeral, the horses were in and night checks and days on the yard became part of the healing ritual.

The last week in February is also Yard Hayley and Martin's birthday's and given the fact that we had been given a Covid exemption certificate and spent the last couple of weeks together in a bubble anyway, I wasn't going to let these amazing people who had been doing everything they could to be there for me not celebrate it. It is in fact in a bid to try and create a fun evening for our group despite what had happened that Martin's infamous party games and pub quizzes were born. He learnt very quickly in his first attempt that 130 questions was perhaps a step too far - falling asleep himself before he got to make his way through giving out all of the answers.

I remember the night as clear as day, my friend Tory had come to stay with me and it was time to start getting ready for the party.

"What are you wearing?" I asked her.

"Little black dress and heels. How about you?"

"I'm not sure, here are my dresses. What do you think?"

She sifted through my wardrobe and pulled out a few tops, grimacing at my clothing choices.

"Your wardrobe is a bit Mumsie. Where's all your killer outfits gone?"

"That is my wardrobe Tory."

I pointed to the clothes in it and grabbed the tops she'd looked at disapprovingly out of her hand.

"But you're not fifty!! Where's your cool, fun stuff gone?"

That's it isn't it, I'd got three small children and had been a wife for the last nine years. I didn't make an effort, I looked exhausted and bedraggled most of the time. Also living with someone with severe mental illness was draining and meant that the little things like self-care and dressing to kill went out of the window. I found a white and black dress I'd had since I was sixteen and put that on. That's one positive I guess of having the physique of a thirteen-year old; no tits, no ass but everyone comments on how skinny you are while you secretly dream of being able to do a Pammy Baywatch run down a beach! But that's it isn't it, nobody is ever satisfied with the way they look and we always think somebody else has it better.

"Right, where's your make up?" Tory rooted through my bathroom cupboard. "That's it." I pointed to a half used bottle of foundation.

"That's it!" She gasped. "Tor! You used to be so glamorous. That's it tomorrow we're sitting down and I'm introducing you to Charlotte Tilbury."

We walked arm in arm round to Martin's cottage with our phone torches on and I felt for the first time the knot in my stomach disappear. As we walked in, I was greeted by my friends' smiling faces and had a glass of wine swiftly placed in my hand. Martin paired everyone into teams and handed out pieces of paper. Round one - Guess who the naked celebrities were by bum and boob pictures only. Laughter filled the room for the first time in over a week as everyone glanced at the pictures. It felt good to laugh and be sociable, which was something during lockdown none of us had been able to do. Being the life and soul of the party, was that also what Matthew had missed being able to do?

I Need Help

Because of Covid and the huge backlog meant that the inquest and coroners court wouldn't be taking place for at least another six months following Matthew's death. An interim death certificate was issued so we could start to close things down that were in his name and begin to plan the dreaded 'F' word and one that I'd been avoiding, the funeral. Once I'd received the interim certificate from the coroner's office I remember sitting down at the computer desk to use the governments 'Tell Us Once' service. Seeing the words 'Deceased' took my breath away and I sat staring at the computer screen in silence for five minutes. The thoughts go through your mind again; I let him die, I should have saved him and now here I am about to plan his funeral.

My sister was a godsend to me and Matthew's parents when it came to planning the funeral. We decided to use the undertakers who had looked after my grandfather so well and felt reassured if they would also take care of Matthew. Alex had received all of the information and made her way over one evening to start making arrangements. We sat down together in the snug and as she started reciting the email to me it suddenly started to feel very real. I couldn't believe I was picking a coffin, a hearse and choosing whether he wanted to be buried or cremated. He hadn't left a will, that's something you do later in life, not at thirty-eight. Alex approached the whole subject very sensitively with me and paused just before she got to the most difficult question. What do you want him to be buried in? What should have been an impossible answer made sense more than ever. The suit he had tried on Valentine's Day was his choice and that was what he was telling me then.

When we finally got a date through for the funeral, the reality had firmly hit that this was now going to happen in ten days, time followed by Bella's birthday only a few days after.

It was at this point I thought 'I know I need help.' When you've experienced trauma, a bereavement, an accident or something that has had a massive effect on you, you know in yourself that you're not ok and deep down that you're struggling. But we all have this big thing called pride that we're afraid to dent the armour of so soldier on for a while with a false smile in public and a broken soul behind closed doors. I reached a point I didn't give a fuck about pride, it was reality that was staring me straight in the face and that I needed to deal with. Yes, it was only three weeks after Matthew had passed, but I had three children who were all sleeping in the same bed as me because all of us were afraid to sleep in our own bedrooms and I had big life decisions to make.

A friend recommended a very good psychotherapist who could help me, obviously the sessions were all going to be online but that meant she could see me fairly sharpish. I logged onto the first Zoom session with her and spent an hour spilling my guts out. I was apprehensive at first and unsure if I was doing the right thing, but it helped me to cast light over the current situation. I didn't want to sit in a room blubbering and psycho analysing my childhood which is what I think automatically comes into peoples heads when you mention counselling, I wanted a matter of fact, non judgmental conversation:

What should I tell the kids to help them come to terms with the situation and how do I help them to deal with everything?

How do I sleep in my bedroom again and get the kids out of my bed?

What should I do about his clothes?

What am I going to do about the business?

These were all questions I asked and we tackled systematically over the next couple of weeks. I ordered canvas pictures for the kids to have in their rooms of them with Daddy and from that moment encouraged them to talk about him with me. We had a small telescope in the house and one evening we sat in front of the window and tried to find the brightest star in the sky.

"That's Daddy," I told them. "Always look for the brightest star in the sky and you can always talk to him or ask him anything."

I found that by encouraging this, they would then suddenly start talking about him or reminiscing good memories. There is obviously still a long way to go, but always encouraging them to be open is a good starting point. We have good days and our fair share of bad ones, particularly with Bella, but their lives still have to feel happy and full of potential at their age as they have the rest of it ahead of them.

When it came to tackling the bedroom scenario, I remember the therapist saying to me.

"You have to go straight back into your bedroom, I know it's not what you want to hear, but you'll never get the kids back into their own bedrooms if you're afraid to go into your own."

I went silent for a few minutes, feeling my heart pound at the thought of it but then realised that

everything she was saying made complete se
I was showing them was that there was sor
sinister in my room, I was making it scary by the way
I approached it. There wasn't a monster in there, a
poltergeist or IT; just a bad memory of a traumatic
experience I associated with that room. It was only
going to bother me if I let it and it was actually just a
case of mind over matter. Before I could tackle the
kids sleeping individually again, I compromised so I
could carry out my task in hand by letting the three
of them sleep together.

"Mummy's sleeping in her bedroom tonight." They
looked at me gone out and almost panicked.

"But why?"

"Because my bed is so comfy and I like my room." I
said through gritted teeth trying my best to convince
them how masculine I was.

I put all of them downstairs and prepared for the
mission in hand. I put the bedside light on, grabbed a
cup of tea and prepared to read a book. As I sat in
bed and looked around the room, I kept telling
myself; 'it's just a room.' I knew I shouldn't, but I
couldn't help myself looking up at the beams.

The book wasn't working, I needed more to occupy
my mind. I went and grabbed my laptop and decided
to update the stud terms and conditions on the
Caunton Stud website. I hadn't paid attention to the

paperwork side of the business for a few weeks, only the physical in our massive tidy up mission. Knowing I was in that room and sat for fifteen minutes thinking of ideas for the business I felt for the first time I'd given myself a positive kick up the arse. 'You can do this!' I told myself. I think we all have to do that from time to time and positive people can help you to do that.

I know some people find it incredibly difficult to empty a wardrobe of clothes or possessions of a loved one, but the reality is the longer you leave it the harder it's inevitably going to get. Those clothes aren't going to bring that person back or remind you of that persons smell. They're going to smell musty and collect dust and just create a section of the wardrobe that you struggle to open. I didn't delay this any further, I knew it needed tackling now. House Hayley arrived to help me when the kids were out the way and we started to make our way through the wardrobes. Matthew was a hoarder anyway so by starting with the ancient, ripped t-shirts seemed like a good way to go. I had no remorse throwing those into black bin liners, as it was a task I'd tried to undertake for quite some years. Matthew favoured the rough cowboy look, occasionally mixed with a splash of Worsel Gummage. There was so much new stuff too still with tags on, so I wanted his closest friends to take what they wanted from that.

"Look at all this stuff Hayley, it's brand new." I held up two cashmere sweaters still in the wrapper.

"Look at it all." I sat down on the bed and felt guilt again. What a waste of life, what a waste of stuff. How could he do this? With suicide there seems to be a divided perception, half think it's selfish and half think it's the bravest thing a person can do. What do I think? Could I do it? Could I walk up to a ledge at the edge of a cliff and see the waves crashing on top of the rocks and bring myself to jump? No, I couldn't do it.

I might have periods where I think life's shit, or I'm feeling enormous amounts of pressure and want to hibernate for a while. But I've learnt to motivate my mind and know how to give myself a big kick when I need one. I think those who can go through with suicide are so unwell it's unfair to cast an opinion as to whether they were brave or selfish. They were not of sound mind and had lost control of their own identity.

I kept one wardrobe of sentimental stuff, Team GB jackets and team kit to show the kids one day part of the legacy that Matthew had left. The rest all went to a Mind charity shop. Although it wasn't a nice task to have undertaken, it felt cleansing that it was done. I think some people thought I'd done that too quickly and couldn't understand why or how I was doing the things I was doing, but after the funeral had taken place, I wanted to be able to close that chapter and move forwards with life and work not just for myself but for my children. When it came to business the therapist was very blunt, she said that people were always going to have opinions or not be particularly pleasant about the decisions I would make because everybody fears change. I was never going to be able to replace my husband or the children's father, but I could replace the dynamics needed to keep the business alive and a business we had worked so hard to create.

I don't think there's any right or wrong answer in how long it takes you to want to start moving forwards again. For me and the type of character I am, I needed to drive at full throttle. For others they may need more time and that's ok too, but you can't be afraid to ever hit the gas again because of the opinions of others who have never walked a day in your shoes.

The Last Goodbye

It was the morning of the Thursday 25th March and I'd set my alarm clock for 7am. Matt and Angus had stayed the night before to spend the night together preparing the eulogy. The last time they'd spent the night together like that was preparing their best man speeches at our wedding. I tried to get an early night and rest and just remember the sun shining through the blinds when I woke up that morning. I walked into the kitchen to make a coffee and looked out of the window across to the paddocks. Angus came upstairs and searched for a kettle, failing to see the zip tap by the sink.

My sister sent me a text to say she was on the way and had a black dress for me to wear, all I needed to do was rest and not start getting ready until she got there. 11am seemed like a long wait ahead, especially when time was stood still. The door beeped and I was greeted by Martin carrying a Starbucks chai latte and some pastries.

"Eat what you want, leave what you don't but if you can try and eat something."

We sat around the island of the kitchen and didn't say that much, silence seemed like the best option at the time. When Alex arrived, she hung the dress on my bedroom door and placed a carrier bag of make up on my bed. "Whenever you feel like you want to start getting ready you can do, I don't want you to feel like you need to rush. Everything is organised you don't need to worry about anything."

I steadily started to get dressed, it was the first time I'd got dressed up in a while, sadly I didn't think it would be in these circumstances. Alex helped me to straighten my hair and do my make up before it was time to wear black. At the time face coverings were compulsory and numbers limited to the church and crematorium. We'd let people know what route the funeral precession was going to take and wanted it to pass through the village Matthew had lived his entire life, past the old yard, past his family home and to the church on the route we always hacked. With Covid, we didn't know if anyone was going to follow, stand outside or even show up.

I wanted Matthew to be taken in a Rolls Royce phantom, the car in which he had raved on about when we stayed at The Savoy in London for our wedding anniversary and with the significance of Valentine's Day, I wanted to make sure the coffin was decorated in red roses. He had always loved extravagance so I wanted to send him off in the way he would have always wanted. That's all you can do at that stage.

Family and friends started to arrive at the house, and I knew it was getting nearer to Matthew's arrival. I sat at the kitchen island and listened to muffled voices as people's conversations were exchanged across the room. My sister and Matt came up the stairs to give the nod that the funeral procession had arrived. Jenny took hold of my hand as everyone left to go outside. I was glued to the chair and literally felt like I couldn't move. Alex put her hands on my shoulders and said it was time to go. I got down from the chair and put one foot in front of the other to walk to the window. The Phantom and undertakers in tailcoats and hats were the first things I saw, followed by the sea of red roses on top of the coffin. I fell backwards into my sisters' arms and Jenny gripped my hand tighter. Tears came flooding out again;

"I can't do this." I started trembling and my teeth were chattering. Matt came across from the top of the stairs and offered his hand out to me.

"Come on Tor, you can do this. We can all go down together."

I took Matts hand and he and Jenny led me down the stairs. As I walked out the door, I remember seeing family and friends lined up outside the house with their heads tipped down. The undertaker opened the doors to the car as myself, Matt, Angus and Alex all stepped in.

I sat between Alex and Matt gripping their hands tightly as the precession rolled out of the drive looking at the air vents near the floor in front of me. When we got into the village all the villagers had lined the streets to pay their respects. The car was silent until we got to the pub at the end of village which had road works and traffic lights in front of them. The light changed to red, causing Matt to break the silence with;

"The fucker just wanted one last trip to the pub."

We all laughed as the car pulled away to the church. I wanted Matthew's closest friends to carry in the coffin, so between Matt, Angus, Chris and James they took on the emotional task of carrying Matthew into the church. I couldn't believe how many people were stood outside, although I never looked up much to take note of who they were. I tried to keep my focus on the floor. We sat down inside and all I could hear were the harrowing tears of Matthew's parents behind me. The service was beautiful and the eulogy read by Angus absolutely perfect. Sometimes there were tears and sometimes laughter, a perfect combination to describe Matthew's life.

The final stage was the drive to the crematorium, breaking point again felt very close at this stage. I remember Alex saying;

"Three things you can see. Three things you can hear and three things you can touch."

As she said this, I noticed Matt touch the roof of the car and knew that he too was needing to find comfort at the same time. The final walk into the crematorium was one of the hardest ones I've had to make. Before saying the last goodbye, Matthew was blown away by the Huntsman's hunting horn as we stood and faced the coffin for one last time. Matt gripped my hand again as we stood up and took small steps to the front.

I had made a pact with all his closest friends to place things on the coffin that Matthew would have wanted to take with him to the end. Never one to be seen without a baseball cap on, I placed his favourite cap on the end of the coffin, House Hayley laid out his chefs apron, Martin rested the horse hair from Amy's tail over the top and Jenny finished it off with his favourite whiskey. We all turned to leave the building and be left only with the memories we had.

Outside the crematorium guests came over to offer condolences and be reunited with friends and family that they hadn't seen for some time. I didn't take the children to the funeral, I took the decision they were too young and were already overwhelmed enough. A private goodbye or memorial ceremony was something we could have at a later date. I desperately needed to get back in the car and get home, I felt emotionally exhausted and nauseous. We had arranged to have the wake back at the new yard around the horses and to be hosted by Matthew's old school friends and favourite restaurant owners. I wanted to send him off in the way he would have wanted and that wasn't going to be with coffee, tea and jugs of orange juice while guests tucked into triangle sandwiches. Wine was on tap, steak and seafood available by the bucket load and the only toast was to be with a nice scotch.

It was like he was looking down on us that day, the sun shone as we sat on hay bales in the stable's car park. We made sure we played his favourite songs and exchanged comical stories that made difficult moments comforting for all involved. It was the last day of doing things Matthew style before the hourglass turned again and tomorrow was another day.

Dealing With Change

I think dealing with change is always a bitter pill to swallow whenever any of us experience a dramatic U-turn in life whether it be through the break up from a long term relationship, the death of a loved one or following a trauma or accident. All we know is that life in our current situation has changed forever and that is a dynamic we are never going to be able to get back. We all hate situations we can't control and in a situation like that it doesn't matter what you do, you're never going to be able to change the circumstances. That change for me was massive because we worked, lived and did everything together and home was our bubble. All of a sudden the bubble becomes a place of uncertainty where you were once so comfortable because that safe haven and space has been demolished by an earthquake.

It becomes all the silly things you then miss about a person; the middle of the night eureka moments of a new bridle combination or why a fence had gone down in the show jumping at 3am which was then your usual cue to go and put the kettle on whilst he searched the internet for what he needed. This conversation used to go on for a good hour before the

TV got put on and we succumbed to Teleshopping, twenty-four hours later a new pressure cooker, steam mop or cooking utensil used to arrive.

Whenever something terrible happens, for the first few weeks everyone is with you, and you never have a minute to think for yourself. It's always after the first few weeks when everyone goes back to living their own lives again, all of that change hits you like a ton of bricks. To start with, you focus on all the negatives of the current situation, the dark times you've had and all the stuff you're not going to be able to do anymore. That's why the mind is such a powerful tool and just because it's in our body and we own it, doesn't mean it's always on our side.

It took me a while to adjust to it just being just me and the kids alone in the house, I had the odd night where Bridget Jones or How To Be Single was played on Netflix because our natural instinct is to always go through a phase where we feel sorry for ourselves and dwell on the fact that everything's so shit. But it's only shit because that's what you're telling yourself.

I was fortunate I had Martin who lived in the cottage around the corner. Martin had also gone through a messy breakup after separating from his long-term partner and was also adjusting to life alone. Once we went through our tracksuit-bottoms-and-ice-cream stage, we realised it's actually possible to make home a safe haven again. We started to see the positives in what we had around us. Living with someone for so many years who struggled with their mental health also meant there were a lot of things you didn't do and socialising and spending quality time with friends didn't happen. When we hit the next phase it was a bit of William Wallace moment; "Ffffrreeeeeeeddddooooommmmmmm!"

I found laughter good for my soul, and although some people that were in different stages of grief themselves around me found that uncomfortable, it was something I needed to do to stitch my heart back together again. After recognising I would need help early on and having received a very matter of fact approach from the therapist who had worked out how I functioned, the stages that a lot of people prolong like clearing out the clothes or dealing with physical things that can be changed straight away, I had already dealt with. The emotional and mental stage was always going to take time, but it's impossible to make a start tidying up any space if you don't remove the clutter first. It's not good to hoard anything and cling onto things that aren't healthy for you, the sooner you can tell your mind to let go of what's bad for you, the closer you are to creating a workspace within it in which you can thrive.

My house has become a bit of an open door now, my friends let themselves in and grab a drink, which is exactly the way I like it. As a new routine developed at home it was still time to adapt to one away from it. Going out for the first time into an environment where everyone knows what's happened is daunting as you become 'that person'. That person who is subject to rumours and 'that person' who's husband has killed himself.

I had decided that I needed to carry on with the competition horses after a walk down to the yard with my father. His forte is motivational pep talks and he delivered one of his best ones yet as we walked into the new barn.

"You know Caunton started originally at home and was always your dream. Just because things are different doesn't mean you need to give up on them."

He was right, just because a big change had happened didn't mean that life had to stop moving forwards. It was exactly just over a month from the funeral when I started to appear in the big wide world again and you find it comes with mixed reactions. Some people come over to show support and ask how you are, while others daren't speak to you because you are 'that person.' You actually start to feel like some people expect you to get back in that corner rocking.

The part I struggled with the most was facing up to the school run again and this was something I put off most of the time. I found it hard in the school environment because you saw parents together, mums and dads as a unit and I was envious of what they had. I also didn't want to highlight that to the kids so avoided it for quite a while. It's almost like some people are afraid to speak to you or feel awkward in doing so. I was also scared to speak up about the ins and outs about what really happened. People might find my house creepy or weird and uncomfortable and not want to let their kids come round to play. I didn't want my children to also become 'those children'. You get isolated from group invites too unless it's specifically a girl's night in which you can go alone, you're certainly not in the couples gang anymore.

I found my own group through this, my tribe, my close family who had been with me through thick and thin and to be honest they were always my people beforehand. I still wanted to live my life, be spontaneous and go out so I did it with my group instead and didn't mind that I became the outcast of other groups. One pact I made with my close group of friends was to continue to turn negatives into positives and the one year anniversary of Matthew's death on Valentine's Day was always going to be hard. Instead of staying at home and letting my mind get the better of me, we made it a day of fun. For me now, it's a case of mind over matter and I don't want to be a victim or have a victim mindset. It will only ever be an issue if I allow it to be.

If you asked me to compare the person I used to be to the person I am now I don't believe I'm any tougher or thicker skinned than I already was. I'd always been pretty tough which was how I survived 2021 in general, that year was tough! Between Matthew, his father and being the first on the scene to a road traffic accident, I'd seen some pretty horrific scenes in the space of six months which all resulted in body bags. I find my tolerance levels much lower if I hear people complaining about first world problems, but equally my door is more open than ever before to sit and talk to people who need help. I certainly feel I have my identity back because I'm no longer silent, when you're silent you only feel more trapped. As soon as you start to open up it's like the weight on your shoulders is lifted too.

It's strange because you spend a year being 'that person' and then all of a sudden, you're just a single parent and new people you meet are unaware of your back story. Do I feel apprehensive telling it to them, of course I do. The memories for me now are locked in a chest and the key in a trinket in my heart, not because I haven't dealt or come to terms with what's happened, but because I can't change the situation. I also can't let my children think that what's happened is going to have a negative impact on their lives and I can do this by showing them it's also not going to stop me living mine. I'd be a liar in saying that I didn't carry an enormous amount of guilt about Matthew, I still think about those fifteen minutes. But it was his choice to do what he did and I view it as the mental equivalent of a heart attack that took him there and then. The darkness of the illness won that night and all I can do now is make it my mission to help find a cure or a way to fight it by finding a clearer path to the light for others.

A huge milestone for me in all the change was deciding when the time was right to take off my wedding ring. After a promise I made to Matthew the evening he died to never remove it, this remained a difficult subject for me for quite some time. I don't think I had ever taken it off in all the years we were married and to even contemplate it now made me feel like I was betraying his wishes. Nobody would even think about it if I was seventy five and had been married for forty years; I'd just leave it on until I passed as well. The difference when you're thirty three and still wearing one with three children aged nine, six and four means that anyone you meet unaware of the situation presumes you're still happily married and the children still have a father.

This isn't easy for anyone following the death of a partner because I think you have this constant battle of 'what if I damage the ring vs they wouldn't want me to take it off. Removal day for me came six months later. I'd revamped the house and made it a family home that had the homely touches I wanted it to have and it certainly felt more feminine than it ever had done before. I'd placed a little jewellery box in the top drawer of my dressing table and subconsciously created a safe space to put it in. I'd revamped my wardrobe too and decided the Mumsie look perhaps needed to be shelved ready for my sixtieth birthday in the not so near future.

I had a shower one evening and remember pouring the shampoo into my hand which drew attention to my ring once again. I was trying to do everything I could to move on with life and create a positive environment to raise the kids in, the ring just didn't fit any part of that anymore. I left the shower and sat on my bed with the towel draped around me and stared into the bedroom mirror. Maybe I can take the ring off for a little bit and see what it feels like. It took me a while to free the ring from my finger and when it finally passed the tip I felt a gut wrenching surge of guilt again. Eventually with time I felt a sense of relief for taking it off and achieving what seemed like such an impossible task at the time. You think something like that is incredibly personal but it's amazing how many people notice you've taken it off.

"Have you taken your wedding ring off?"

"Yes."

"Oh!" Which was usually followed by raised eyebrows insinuating you must have moved on or secretly got married in Vegas. But the reality is only you know the right time to do something like that and it's irrelevant what anyone else thinks.

The Toll On The Children

The effects on the children showed in different ways and at different stages. When everything first happened, they didn't cry that much because the information wasn't absorbed, they hadn't experienced loss before so probably still kept hope in the back of their heads that Daddy might still come back. Slowly over time he would pop up in random conversations when I least expected it and it was either a question or a memory shared. I remember William asking me while we were unpacking the food shopping;

"Mummy, what actually happened to Daddy?"

"Well, you know how he was very poorly and had been poorly for a long time?"

"I didn't know he was poorly." William looked me straight in the eye as Niamh and Bella quickly followed suit intrigued as to what my answer would be.

"We didn't tell you how poorly he was because we didn't want to worry you at the time and we weren't sure if he was going to get better. The doctors tried to save Daddy but couldn't, now what we have to do is try and help as many poorly people as we can get better. One day you'll understand a lot more about illness and you'll be able to help lots of people too. That's what Daddy would want us all to do."

I have explained things to them in this way because of the work we do with our equestrian mental health charity Riders Minds. Matthew's legacy to the sport he loved and to his children, will be an example of how to take something negative, turn it into something positive and hopefully help other people also struggling with it. Bella and William certainly seemed to show the more obvious signs of grief in the early days, mainly becoming hermits at home. Bella in particular, was always very sporty and involved in every activity at school and with her ponies at home. When Matthew passed this stopped very abruptly and she lost all self-confidence not having her idol there, particularly in sport. I remember taking her cross country running at school and her crying on the way back in the car because she finished in the middle of the field.

"I'm not good enough anymore, I can't do it."

"You can't think like that Bella, you can achieve anything."

Because she'd got this into her mind, her comfort zone in anything had disappeared and she had filled herself with self-doubt. William to some extent had also mirrored her behaviour and didn't want to do anything either. Although you encourage them to do activities, you also remain soft and if they don't want to do something you don't make them and take the approach they'll get better in time.

This actually does them no good either, it gets to a point you have to play bad cop and I became someone they didn't like. Getting them back out into the open world again was tough and I know that they too struggled seeing other children have both parents there to support on the sidelines when they took part in a school activity or at sports day. But what you have to be very clear about is that there are actually lots of other children out there who live with only one parent, either through separation or from being a bereaved family. They are not the odd ones out and you can still have all the love and support in the world from the great people around them. I stopped instantly my dislike of making an appearance at school and realised that it's easy to create issues for them to follow; around children you always have to be incredibly thoughtful about your actions.

I actually made a bucket list in the end, a priority on there was to make all three of my children worldly and to instil a good work ethic into all of them as my parents had done for me. This year in particular kicking their arse and getting them out the house to try new things and see the world, which was encouraged by a great friend, was the best thing I did.

"I hate you!"

"Meany!"

"Why do you hate me?"

These were all of the expressions delivered to me by my tribe as a result of it and it's hard hearing those words when you think they've been through so much already. You want to back off and hug them and tell them don't worry there's always another day, but what does that achieve? You're then just telling them that quitting is ok and how to be a victim themselves. We continued to make them do the things they didn't want to do, only to find eight hours later they have embraced every opportunity with open arms, taken on new hobbies and activities and found confidence again in everything they do. There's still a long way to go, but sometimes you have to be the person they don't like to help snap them out of that negative mindset. Children at a young age are heavily influenced and can learn to play the wave the white flag card when things are tough anyway.

One of the biggest hurdles faced in dealing with change with children is when the whole family isn't at the same stage when it comes to moving forwards. After seeking help and making a plan to move on myself, the tasks I faced like the clothes and belongings around the house were straight forward when it was only me that needed to deal with them. Over time, the wedding pictures, family photos of all of us in it staring at you in the face every day can also become an unhealthy reminder. I had obviously put a canvas in each of the kids rooms which was a picture of them with Daddy, but I wanted to start to put more recent pictures around the house that resembled life now and all the great things they were doing. It came with challenges, especially from Bella who took a while to accept them. She saw it as though I was trying to get rid of the memories of him, but that was because she herself was clinging onto the past and the hope he may one day miraculously walk back through the door.

She still wrote a lot of letters to him and got angry if I found them. Our relationship suffered for a while when I kept forcing her out of the house and wouldn't allow her to become a hermit. The dynamics changed instantly when I became the only parent, I was always the softer touch compared to Matthew and this took a lot of adjusting to for all three of the children. The motherly role and soft touch was taken on by house Hayley, leaving me as the final say and disciplinarian. Whats strange is when it's just me and them left in the house, I become

Mum again and they allow me to shower them with affection. It's a nice balance this way and although never the ideal situation we plan when we have children, is an ideal one that works now given the circumstances. That's all you can do, find dynamics that work to bring them up in the best environment possible.

We put all the pictures in the snug and created one room in the house that the kids can go into if they want to feel close to Daddy. Even now this still needs adapting as ironically it's a room they don't use that often, mainly because I think there are too many pictures and reminders in there. It's the kind of room you expect the crazy lady with the cats to have and are permanently waiting for dozens of felines to surround you when you go in there. Over a year later, they're now at a stage they'd still like some pictures in there, but want it to be more of a sociable hang out they can sit in with friends. It just takes them a little while longer to realise too much memorabilia in one room can become oppressive.

The children were offered support straight away from the Tomorrow project and the Children's Bereavement Centre, but I found when they're only young you have to go with the daily flow of what they need on each particular day. Sometimes they want to talk and sometimes they don't, but the key point for me was the importance of making them feel normal. They shouldn't feel different to any other child and at that age in a school environment, the importance of fitting in really matters to them. Not creating a victim mentality is so important and you should never use the situation as an excuse yourself so they don't learn to either.

Dealing with every challenge that life can throw and being prepared for anything is something I want to teach my children. I also want them to be aware of what a powerful tool the mind is and to learn to understand and control it. I think children should be under no illusions how tough life can be, we can't protect them forever, but we can make life more fulfilling for them by teaching them how to protect themselves. Competition is natural, but it's having the desire to improve, to want to learn and to accept that you will lose at certain points in life, but that doesn't mean you should quit that's important. Failure is the first attempt in learning after all and it's through failure that we learn to do things better than we did before. You can't dwell on failure either, this isn't healthy and this was always the unhealthy place Matthew stayed in. Even when you're having a bad day, it is only ever a bad day, tomorrow will always be a new one with brand new possibilities all over again.

"When everything seems to be going against you remember that an airplane takes off against the wind, not with it."   – Henry Ford-

Afterthought

Do I think the pressures of life killed Matthew, was it the sport he was involved in or the fact we were in the middle of a global pandemic at the time and he felt once again like a caged bird; a phrase he would often use to describe an early part of his life. Or was it a combination of everything?

When the inquest finally took place nine months later, Matthew's cause of death was confirmed and the death certificate released. Cause Of Death - Suicide caused by asphyxia (hanging). I would rather this said mental health or mental illness than suicide and hanging; maybe people would talk about it more openly if it did.

The sport is tough, gruelling and cruel at times as well as being elating, inspiring and great; it usually just depends if it's your lucky time within it. But I think any sport is tough at a professional level and always has been. Years ago, following a bad result or bout of bad luck we used to just not pick up the newspaper or magazine it was featured in. Instead in today's modern society, everything is plastered all over social media and people's opinions broadcast publicly to everyone in an alarmingly dangerous way. I believe it can be a very powerful marketing tool but also an equally powerful depressant that needs far more regulation.

During the pandemic the suicide rate was at its highest because freedom and regular life was taken away from people, but were these people already struggling? And if so many are already struggling, what creates such a huge barrier that stops them seeking support and getting help?

The cost of living is now extortionate and the expectations of society extremely high, are we not highlighting enough to young people that the real world is actually fucking tough and it's hard to make a living in it. Therefore, we should be teaching them how to be prepared for it instead of protecting them the entire time?

These are all questions that constantly go through my head as I hear daily of another person gone too soon. The subject of mental health is real and is a problem that needs tackling and tackling right now, but is certainly one that cannot be tackled alone.

I urge everyone to never take anything for granted and to always think before making a judgment on somebody or passing negative comment. It's impossible to see what's going on inside someone's head and even if you think you know, I can assure you have no idea.

Happiness Can Be Found In The Darkest Of Places If One Only Remembers To Turn On The Light.

-Dumbledore-

Printed in Great Britain
by Amazon

85731724R00047